The FACT ATTACK series

Awesome Aliens
Beastly Bodies
Cool Cars
Crazy Creatures
Crucial Cricket
Dastardly Deeds
Deadly Deep
Devastating Dinosaurs
Dreadful Disasters
Fantastic Football
Gruesome Ghosts
Incredible Inventions
Mad Medicine
Magnificent Monarchs
Nutty Numbers
Remarkable Rescues
Rowdy Rugby
Spectacular Space
Super Spies
Vile Vampires

FACT ATTACK

SUPER SPIES

IAN LOCKE

MACMILLAN CHILDREN'S BOOKS

First published 1999 by Macmillan Children's Books

This edition published 2012 by Macmillan Children's Books
a division of Macmillan Publishers Limited
20 New Wharf Road, London N1 9RR
Basingstoke and Oxford
Associated companies throughout the world
www.panmacmillan.com

ISBN 978-1-4472-2443-3

1 3 5 7 9 8 6 4 2

A CIP catalogue record for this book is available from
the British Library.

Printed and bound by CPI Group (UK) Ltd, Croydon CR0 4YY

DID YOU KNOW THAT . . .

 Some of the earliest spies are in the Bible. Moses used twelve spies to go ahead of the Israelites on their way to the Promised Land.

 One of the best-known of the early English spies was King Alfred the Great. According to legend, he disguised himself as a harp-player and walked into his enemies' camps to pick up information.

1

Names of the Secret Services:
CIA: Central Intelligence Agency (USA)
KGB: Soviet intelligence service (former USSR)
MI6: British secret intelligence service
OURA: The Italian secret service
FIA: The German secret service
Mossad: The Israeli secret service overseas
ASIS: Australian Secret Intelligence Services
ONI: The Office of Naval Intelligence (USA)
SDECE: The French secret service
SIFAR: The Italian counter-espionage service

Daniel Defoe, the writer famous for *Robinson Crusoe*, who worked for a time as a butcher, became an English government secret agent. He got on well enough to become friends with King William III.

When actor Sean Connery, the original movie James Bond, joined the Scottish National Party he was given the membership number 007!

 Sir Anthony Blunt, a well-known British art historian who looked after the Queen's pictures, was found in the 1960s to have spied for Russia for many years.

 An English spy, who became the Duchess of Portsmouth, is recorded to have earned a fortune for her information. In 1681 alone she received £138,668 – worth up to £100 million today!

 The Man from UNCLE was first shown on American TV on 22 September 1964. The name of the lead character, Napoleon Solo, was thought up by the man who created James Bond – Ian Fleming.

The American K-12 spy satellite is believed to be so good that it can photograph objects as small as 15 centimetres from space!

Every modern battle has a code. 'Hail Mary' was the code used for the coalition forces in the move against the Iraqi armies in the Gulf War.

Sir Francis Walsingham, the master of spies in England for Elizabeth I, paid for the spies himself. It made him bankrupt and he died in poverty in 1590.

The American CIA agent Martha Petersen used a piece of hollowed-out coal to pass messages to spies in Moscow.

Einstein, the great German-American scientist, was friendly with a number of women. Among his closest friends was a Russian, Margarita Konenkova. What Einstein did not know was that she was a spymaster.

 During the Cold War, East German agents used an infra-red beam to send messages from the East to West Germany.

 The weapons for secret agents can be tiny. The Soviets made a lipstick that held a real 4 mm gun!

Spy Harry Gold, who worked for the
Russians, was awarded the Order of the
Red Star. When he was released from an
American jail in 1965 he died before he
could use one of the perks of the award –
free rides on Moscow buses.

 Women are searched less often than
men. As a result, female spies can
be more effective than men.

 After the Cold War ended in 1989,
many spies were able to go home.
One of the most recent to go back was
Polish spy Colonel Kuklinski. He went
back to Poland in 1998, after spending
17 years in the United States.

The British major John André, on a secret
service mission during the American War of
Independence in 1780, was caught by the
Americans. In his riding boot, documents
were found which showed the details of
the American defences around West Point,
an American fortress. In court André was
found guilty of espionage and sentenced to
death. Forty years after he died, his remains
were brought back to England and buried
with full honours in Westminster Abbey.

 From the 1940s to the 1980s there were
150,000 informers in East Germany.

 Mokomoko, a chief of the Maori
tribe, was pardoned in New Zealand
in 1992. He had been hanged
126 years before for murdering a
missionary, Carl Volkner, whom the
Maoris suspected of spying for the
British.

During World War II, the famous
underwater explorer Jacques Cousteau
posed as an ordinary diver in the south
of France – while working as a secret
agent. His job was to monitor Nazi naval
movements.

 100,000 agents worked for the East
German security police, the Stasi.

 If a soldier in uniform is caught
on a secret mission behind enemy
lines he or she is usually treated as
a prisoner of war. If the soldier is in
civilian clothes, they can be tried
as a spy and, often, face the death
penalty.

The first headquarters of the British secret service bureau was at 2 Whitehall Court, London. If they were still there now they'd be just around the corner from McDonald's!

 In 1776, American army officer Nathan Hale was sent on a secret mission behind British lines in the American War of Independence. He was dressed as a Dutch schoolmaster. After being betrayed by an American who recognized him, he was tried by a British court martial and found guilty of spying. Because he was in civilian clothes, he was hanged. He became a legend to the Americans.

When Genghis Khan and his forces invaded Europe in the 13th century, he knew what to expect. He had recruited spies who posed as merchants and traders. The information reached him in under 24 hours by using a string of ponies. Normally such a journey would have taken ten days. Genghis Khan's arrangements were not forgotten. The idea of using a string of horses for quick delivery of messages was revived in the US Wild West hundreds of years later – as the Pony Express!

 East Germany sold 33,000 prisoners for 3.4 billion Deutschmarks during the 1970s and 1980s. They used the money to buy technology from the West.

 Soviet spy Emma Woikin passed on secrets in the lavatory of her dentist – they were collected by a chauffeur.

There are no friends in spying. In July 1998 three Germans went on trial in Germany because they had bought Russian military secrets for Britain, not Germany.

 The American CIA once put together a special copy of the popular magazine *National Geographic*. On the edge of an advert was printed a tiny message in code. The Russian agent who received it was able to read the message under a microscope.

 The famous English playwright Christopher Marlowe was said to have been murdered by three agents of Sir Francis Walsingham in a pub in Deptford, London, in 1593, after it was found that he was plotting against Queen Elizabeth I.

When a bomb exploded in a Munich beer cellar where Hitler was supposed to be holding a meeting, he blamed the British MI6. Hitler had left early, but six others were killed and 60 injured. The Nazi SS then kidnapped two British agents and they were taken to Berlin.

 The secret codes used by the Germans in the 19th century were inspired by the American horror and detective story writer Edgar Allan Poe.

 After the Japanese attack on Pearl Harbor, American code-breakers cracked the Japanese Purple Code. This work was vital in helping the US forces defeat the Japanese in the Battle of Midway in May 1942, changing the course of the war.

Karel Richter, a World War II German spy, was caught after parachuting down near St Alban's, Hertfordshire. He could not explain why he was wearing three sets of underwear and two pairs of socks on a warm summer evening!

 The British film star David Niven became an espionage agent during World War II. He spoke fluent German and is said to have taken part in raids behind enemy lines.

 Many countries release state secrets 30 or 50 years after the event. The secrets are sometimes surprising. It is now known that in the 1960s the US made a light nuclear bomb for carrying around a battlefield. They also tested a nuclear bazooka – called the Davy Crockett.

One part of the British spy system –
MI5, for home operations – used to
be entirely secret. Now the number is
in the telephone book and Directory
Enquiries give it out quite happily.

 World War II British agent Wing
Commander Forest Yeo-Thomas
was known as the 'White Rabbit'. An
exceptionally brave individual, he worked
for the Special Operations Executive (SOE)
in France. He once escaped from the
Germans by hiding in a coffin!

 The American spy Christopher Boyce
escaped from jail on 21 January 1980.
He had been jailed for selling plans for
spy satellites and CIA documents to the
Soviets. He was on the run for over 19
months in America, during which time he
became a master of disguise and robbed
at least thirteen banks.

John Thurlow, an Essex lawyer, was given £70,000 by Cromwell to set up a network of spies in 1645.

 Britain had no organized spy service from 1660 to 1914.

 The real name of the famous World War I spy Mata Hari was Margaretha Geertruida Zelle. She was very stylish: she ordered a new suit and gloves to wear at her execution in 1917.

 German master spy Johann Steiber died in 1892. Many important people in Europe attended his funeral – just to be sure this man whom they feared was really dead.

In US libraries you can read a magazine produced for spies and those who work in the intelligence services quite openly.

 In the 1940s a spy camera was made from a lighter. It really worked!

 Robert Lee Johnson, a US GI, was given a lock-picking computer by the Russians in 1962 to enable him to get into the 'impregnable' armed forces security centre at Orly airport in Paris. He had to be careful since the computer was radioactive. On 16 December 1962 he used the combination to open the safe and take out highly secret documents. It took him just two minutes to open the three locks – the plan worked perfectly.

During World War I, German secret agents caught in Britain were found to have used hankies covered in secret writing to receive their instructions.

 Of the top ten films of all time shown on British TV up until 1998, four were James Bond films. *The Spy Who Loved Me* was watched by 22.9 million viewers when it was first shown on 28 March 1982.

 Britain's modern intelligence service was established under Captain Vernon Kell on 23 August 1909. It was called MO5 before the name was changed to MI5.

 The British spy Sidney Reilly, known as the 'Ace of Spies', worked as a docker, a roadmender and a cook on an expedition to the Amazon before he became a super-spy.

During the 1960s Belgian spies used a toilet in a train as a place to leave messages!

 In November 1993 the American CIA decided it could allow the sale of pictures taken by US spy satellites. The value of the business was put at a huge $1 billion!

 In 1998, to mark its 50th anniversary, the CIA opened a kids' page on the Internet. It was called the *ABC of Spying* and included a list of books to read. These included *The First Book of Codes and Ciphers* and the more unusual title *The US Frogmen of World War II*.

Reilly, the British spy known as the 'Ace of Spies', went back to Moscow in 1925. Nothing more was heard of him. Although his wife stated in a newspaper ad that he had been killed by Russian troops, this was not certain. In World War II it was said that Reilly had really been helping the Russians and in 1972 a Paris newspaper claimed that he had always been a Soviet agent. What happened to Reilly remains a mystery.

 Britain could make a real mess of spying. In the 1940s the man they put in charge of spying on the Russians, Kim Philby, was already a spy for the Russians!

 Frank Brossard, a British spy at the Ministry of Aviation, was caught because MI5 had put tiny tracking bleepers on files. He'd taken some of them out of the building and was traced to a hotel room. He ended up being jailed for 25 years.

The British spy George Blake was sentenced to a record 42 years in jail in 1961. On 22 October 1967, helped by three cellmates, he was able to escape from Wormwood Scrubs prison by kicking out weakly cemented bars on a window in his cell. He then vanished, only to turn up in Moscow, where he still lives.

 In the 1980s the British government tried to ban the book *Spycatcher* by former agent Peter Wright. By 1994 it had sold 12 million copies.

 The 1960s TV series *The Man from UNCLE* was a huge hit. UNCLE stood for United Network Command for Law Enforcement.

 America's first pilotless spy plane, the UAV Dark Star, was launched over the Mojave desert, California, in April 1996.

On 24 September 1971, 105 Russian diplomats and four members of the trade delegation were kicked out of Britain for spying.

 The Americans were busy with German spies in World War II. One group of spies was sentenced to 320 years in jail; another bunch went to jail for 132 years.

 After he defected from the USSR in 1971, Oleg Lyania had plastic surgery to change his looks and avoid being hunted down by the KGB.

 John Dee, who was an astrologer and a secret agent for Queen Elizabeth I, signed himself 007 – 400 years before James Bond.

In 1967 fake 'top secret' documents were printed to advertise a new book by the author Len Deighton. They were so realistic that the FBI was called in to investigate. Some time later they were dumped in a bin in New York. Found by a Slav, he took them to the Russians at the United Nations and asked $100,000 for them. The Russians almost paid up!

 During the 1960s spies would have had terrible trouble at the Ile de Levant in France – half the area was a testing ground for French rockets, the other half was a nudist colony!

Sometimes a story can be close to the truth. Nicholas Luard, who owned part of the magazine *Private Eye*, wrote a story about terrorism which was so real that the CIA suspected that one of their operators had leaked the whole story. During their investigation they bought lots of copies of Luard's book.

 One of the traditional 'covers' for British spies was the job of passport control officer.

 In 1992 a triangular hypersonic US spy plane was said to exist. It cost up to $10 billion! It was said to be able to reach anywhere on Earth in under three hours.

Erskine Childers became famous for the spy book *The Riddle of the Sands*. It was about a planned German invasion of Britain and came out in 1900. The book began a real spy operation and in 1910 two British agents were caught by the Germans. Thrown in jail, they were only released when the German leader, Kaiser Wilhelm, gave them a pardon when George V visited Germany. Childers ran out of luck in 1922: he was declared a traitor by both the British and Irish during the civil war and executed by firing squad.

 Books can change history and can be deadly! In 1959 the American author Richard Condon wrote a spy novel, *The Manchurian Candidate*. Many still believe it to be the inspiration for the assassination of President Kennedy in 1963.

The spywriter Nigel West was, until the 1997 British election, a Conservative MP for Torbay in Devon.

 Miles Copeland, the father of the drummer in the 1980s band The Police, worked as a spy with the American OSS and CIA up to the 1950s.

 The British writer Graham Greene worked as a spy during World War II.

 Among the rarest spy cameras were two made to look like Lucky Strike cigarette packets. They were made in the USA in 1949.

The Russians were worried about the success of James Bond in the 1960s. They were delighted when a Bulgarian came out with a book in which spy Avakum Zakhov and the Russians beat Bond. The only problem was, in the whole book they were not allowed to use the name Bond or the number 007!

 A Victorian spy camera was only one inch (2.5 cm) across and was disguised as a lady's opera glass. It was sold for £23,100 in 1991.

The British spy writer Bernard Newman, who was a relative of the famous Victorian novelist George Eliot, always kept his eyes open and ears listening. While on holiday in Germany in 1938 he made an amazing discovery. He came across some unusual concrete buildings surrounded by barbed wire. A hotel keeper was able to tell him that the place was used for testing big new rockets. Newman thought this was important and told the British secret service; they didn't think much of the story and did nothing about it. A few years later, the rockets – the V2s – began to devastate parts of London.

 In Japan to be a spy is a good job. Spies were even listed in the telephone and postal directories in the 1890s.

Ronald Seth became a British spy in Estonia in World War II. He was parachuted in with enough explosives to blow up a whole town and told to destroy the oil fields being used by the Nazis. He landed right in the middle of a German patrol! His radio and explosives were taken away, but he managed to escape. He was captured after twelve days as a spy. Beaten up, he was sentenced to hang. An unknown Estonian fixed the gallows so it wouldn't open and he was saved! He was never taken to the gallows again and managed to fool the Germans into believing he was a double agent.

 One area where the Japanese secret service leads the world is very unusual – underwater surveillance!

 The American CIA has a private air service, known as CAT.

The Chinese were able to discover about the atom bomb quicker than expected because there were over 3,500 Chinese students at college in the USA. Some were able to find out about the bomb through their studies.

 Over the years, spies have developed their own language. Some of the more unusual words used include:

Doctor – the police

Cobbler – a forger of false passports

Hospital – prison

Shoe – false passport

Soap – truth drug

Measles – a murder which looks like death from natural causes, such as illness or an accident

Lion-tamer – a muscle man used to 'soften up' enemies

New Zealand's secret service remained secret until 1985. It then sent out its first ever report.

 Only one American soldier was found guilty of spying during the Gulf War. Albert Somboloy, aged 40, was caught spying for Iraq and Jordan. He was sentenced at Fort Leavenworth, Kansas, to 34 years in jail in December 1991.

 British spies have their own club in London – it is called the Special Forces Club.

 There are two sorts of spying: basic intelligence, where the agent works for his or her own country; and counter-intelligence, where the agent tries to prevent the work of 'enemy' agents in all areas.

A 'spy university' was set up at Lund University in Sweden about forty years ago.

 Great success as a spy can sometimes depend on very small things. During World War II, the British were fighting the Italians in the deserts of North Africa. One day a British agent, the son of the religious leader the Aga Khan, came across the shell of a bullet. When he looked at it he realized that it was marked with a letter that did not appear in the Italian alphabet, but did appear in the German alphabet. Italian guns could not fire German bullets. This evidence confirmed that the German leader Hitler had begun to send troops to North Africa.

When a spy decides to go over to the enemy (or the other side), he or she is known as a defector. A lot of trouble is taken to make sure these people are safe and able to pass over their information. Almost all defectors are taken to 'safe houses' to tell their story. Later many defectors will be given new identities, places to live and jobs where no one suspects what they might have done in the past.

 During World War II, the British Scout Association was thought by some German leaders to be a spying organization.

Thomas Beach became a British spy by accident when in the USA. It all started with a $20 note he found in 1865, with 'Irish Republic' stamped on it. He realized that this was used by Irish people to try and start a separate Irish state. He worked at trying to stop this happening.

 The CIA headquarters are at Langley, Virginia. There is no clue as to what the buildings really are. For a long time the only notice to the place was a sign saying Bureau of Public Roads, so it was known as BPR. The headquarters is now known as the Fairbanks Highway Research Station.

 Sir Richard Burton, the great Victorian explorer, worked as a spy. When in India, he was so good at his disguise as an Indian that often his commanding officer did not recognize him.

Pierce Brosnan became James Bond in 1995. By coincidence the first full-length book on the Bond films, *James Bond in the Cinema*, was written by John Brosnan in 1972.

Englishman James Holman went blind in 1810. A few years later he was expelled from Russia on suspicion of spying!

The name of the secret service in Iraq is the Listening Post.

The Soviet agent Petrov became really interested in soccer matches in Australia, saying, 'This is a spendid game. I should be quite happy to stay in your country for ever.' He must have been happy, since he decided to stay in Australia and tell the Australians all he knew.

Ten people who have been spied on by the CIA or FBI:

1. John Lennon, the Beatles singer
2. Frank Sinatra, the singer
3. The Duke of Windsor, former British king
4. Princess Diana
5. George Raft, American film star
6. Paul Newman, American film star
7. President J. F. Kennedy
8. Martin Luther King, civil rights campaigner
9. Bob Dylan, singer
10. Harry Belafonte, singer

 James Angleton, who was head of the CIA counter-intelligence, was an expert on orchids and loved poetry.

 When there was an attempt to assassinate Pope John Paul II in Rome in 1981, two Bulgarian agents were believed to be part of the plot.

Cardinal Richelieu, the French politician who also appeared in the famous book *The Three Musketeers*, set up a big spy network in France. It was known as the *Cabinet Noir*.

 Agents who work for MI5 cannot arrest anyone. They have to ask the police.

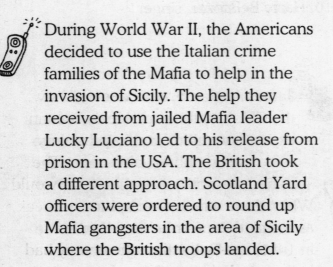 During World War II, the Americans decided to use the Italian crime families of the Mafia to help in the invasion of Sicily. The help they received from jailed Mafia leader Lucky Luciano led to his release from prison in the USA. The British took a different approach. Scotland Yard officers were ordered to round up Mafia gangsters in the area of Sicily where the British troops landed.

False or untrue information is often sent out or publicized by agents to fool the other side. This stuff is called disinformation.

 Around 1950, 80,000 people were recruited by the Hungarian intelligence. The whole population was only 9.5 million! This was a huge number – it would be like recruiting about 500,000 people in Britain.

 In the 18th century Antoine Rossignol in France decided how codes should work. He thought that it would never be possible to devise an unbreakable code. The best possible code, therefore, would be one which took so long to break that the information would be useless by the time the enemy had decoded it.

Two British spies caught in Germany in 1913 had to pay for their own trial. It cost them £380 each!

 One of the biggest threats to national security is now the computer hacker. In July 1998 in San Francisco, a team using a $250,000 special computer cracked the US government codes in 56 hours. The computer had 1,800 chips.

 MI5, the British agency, sometimes goes a bit mad. In the 1950s there was a plan to create a disease in the baobab tree of Africa. The baobab – the 'upside-down tree' – was sacred to the Kikuyu tribe of Kenya. The plan was to plant the disease in Kenyan trees and make the members of the tribe believe that the gods did not approve of their support for the Mau Mau terrorists! The plot was a complete failure – the tribe was far too clever.

The largest computer system in Europe is said to be run by NATO in Cheltenham to crack codes.

 To identify themselves, Venetian secret agents of the 1400s had the insignia 'CDX' woven by a special process into the insides of their black cloaks.

 Sir Noel Martin-Macfarlane came up with a plan to personally assassinate Hitler in 1938, with a shot from a flat he had in Berlin. The British secret service and Government rejected the plan.

 The ancient Romans used pigeons for carrying messages.

Ten famous real or alleged spies of the 20th century:
1. Cary Grant, movie star
2. Noel Coward, British writer
3. Walt Disney, movie maker
4. David Niven, movie star
5. Rex Harrison, movie star
6. Lucky Luciano, US crime boss
7. Robert Maxwell, tycoon and criminal
8. The Aga Khan, religious leader
9. The Duchess of Windsor, wife of former British king
10. Errol Flynn, movie star

 The South Korean spy organization is known as KISS.

 The head of the British secret service (or SIS) is known as 'C'. The first C was Sir Mansfield Cumming. He lost a leg after a car accident. He moved around the office by putting his artificial wooden leg on a scooter and scooting about!

The German spy Lody managed to believe a rumour that Russian soldiers had landed in Scotland. Thinking that Russian troops were about to cross the Channel, the Germans did not send in all their troops in the Battle of the Marne in 1914. The Germans lost the battle as a result.

At the age of 16 John Ramensky, from Glasgow, was detained for theft. Off and on he was to spend 40 years of his life in jail. But he had his moment of glory. He was an expert at opening safes. In 1942 he was hired as an agent by the Government. He was sent to Italy to blow safes and steal German plans. On one mission at the German embassy in Rome he managed to open four strongrooms and ten safes in hours! Not long after he returned home he was back to normal work and was soon in jail again.

The magician and spy for Elizabeth I, John Dee, warned about the Spanish plan to attack English forests before the Armada. The attack was to stop the trees being used for new English ships. Dee said he knew of the plot by talking to an angel called Madini!

 Henri Curiel, the uncle of the British spy George Blake, was also a spy. He was shot dead by terrorists in France in May 1978. He had spied for the KGB and helped some of the world's worst terrorists, including Carlos the Jackal.

 The couple Reinhard and Sonja Schulze worked as spies for the East Germans. Their main office was their garden shed at their home in Cranford, Middlesex! They were caught and both jailed for ten years in July 1986.

There was a bit of a problem in Spain in 1984. One part of the security services was spying on another!

 When MI5 tested 200 agents with a lie detector in 1985, 74 of them failed!

 Allan Pinkerton, the organizer of the first modern intelligence agency in America and of the Pinkerton Detective Agency, was not American. He was born in Glasgow.

 Daniel Defoe, the author of *Robinson Crusoe*, was a spy for England's Queen Anne and King George I.

Why not have your own spies? During the 1970s the head of the Swiss intelligence service organized his own private spies in Austria. Found out, he was sacked.

 Trebitsch Lincoln was one of the most dotty spies. He was nearly always useless and short of money. But he spied for Britain, Germany (twice), a Chinese warlord, China, Tibet and possibly Ceylon (Sri Lanka) up to the 1940s. He was said to be dead in 1943, but in 1947 was reported alive in Sri Lanka. He was also a priest, a Buddhist monk, a journalist . . . and was jailed as a con man!

 Sir Edward Stafford was the first known double agent in history. He spied for England and Spain in Tudor times.

The British spy and ambassador Sir Henry Wotton, who lived from 1568 to 1639, knew the job he had. He stated, 'An ambassador is an honest man sent to lie abroad for the good of his own country.'

Ten films and TV series which include intelligence agents:

1. *The Spy Who Came in from the Cold* (film)
2. *It Takes a Thief* (TV series)
3. *The FBI* (TV series)
4. *The X-Files* (TV series)
5. *Tinker, Tailor, Soldier, Spy* (TV series and film)
6. *Mission: Impossible* (TV series and film)
7. *Funeral in Berlin* (film)
8. *The Prisoner* (TV series)
9. *The Third Man* (film)
10. *Ice Station Zebra* (film)

A spy can be a legend in his or her own lifetime. In spy language, a 'legend' is a faked life, or new identity. Spies have to get used to the details of being a completely different person.

in April 1986, the former vice-president of Sudan, who'd helped the CIA, was sentenced to life in jail (twice) and fined 24 million Sudan pounds for his work!

Taiwan often used members of the Chinese criminal organization the Triads as spies. There were 18 groups of the 14K Triads used as spies in Hong Kong in 1949.

During the 1960s it was rumoured that the UK Labour Party leader Hugh Gaitskell had been poisoned by the KGB so that Harold Wilson, said to be a Soviet agent, could take over. The CIA almost believed the story.

 For a short time during World War II, the head of the British Special Operations Executive, which looked after agents abroad and tasks like blowing up railways, was known as 'M'. Ian Fleming used the letter for the spy boss in the James Bond books.

 Sometimes stories can help in the real world. The US author Leon Uris wrote a story called *Topaz*. In the book he hinted that there were Soviet spies high up in France. The French decided to look. They caught spy Georges Paques. He was jailed for life for passing top NATO secrets to the Russians.

When a spy or agent is tested on a lie detector, the experience is known as being fluttered.

 A radio operator in a spy network is often known as a musician.

 For about ten years MI5 has had a new name – DI5 – but everyone still uses the old name.

 Sir John Rennie, head of MI6 in the 1950s, made his name as a painter. His pictures were shown at the Royal Academy and in Paris.

In the late 1960s, the Russians and the Czechs had a plan to close down the London Underground and cut off London's water supply.

A place where secret messages are left is known as a drop. Some of them are fairly obvious – like holes in walls, or gaps in a flight of steps. Some drops can be marked with a secret chalk mark.

In February 1986 the Israelis claimed that Carlos the Jackal, the world's most infamous terrorist and spy, had been killed and buried in the Libyan desert. A very much alive Carlos was jailed over ten years later in Paris.

Jules Silber, a German spy in World War I, worked in Britain as a censor of letters. One day a woman's letter caught his eye. She had written that her brother was working on secrets for the Navy. Silber went to see her. He pretended to be a British security officer. He told her what she did was wrong and that to avoid trouble she should tell him everything she knew about what her brother did. She did so. As a result Silber was able to pass on secrets about the Royal Navy's new 'Q' ships to the Germans. Silber was never found out. When he left his job as censor, all his office gave him a party. They never thought they were saying goodbye to a spy!

Among the spies used by the Russians and Americans were caretakers and cleaners. Cleaners could often find important information in rubbish. In America, the traitor and spy for the Russians, Aldrich Ames, was caught by, among other things, a careful look at his rubbish bins.

 Before the Israeli Mossad security officers went ahead with the rescue of over 100 hostages held by terrorists in Entebbe, Uganda, in 1976, they used astrology to check that the timing was right.

 The best escape routes for British agents and prisoners of war during World War II were organized by an office in London called MI9. The Germans had their own escape routes. These became known as 'rat lines'. Many Nazi war criminals made their escape down these lines after the war. They later turned up in South America.

Humint is human intelligence (information from people). Electronic intelligence, from bugs, spy planes, spy satellites, and so on, is known as Elint.

 For many years people have been watched by the security services all over the world. In the USA and other places, simple information like shopping lists, names, addresses, and purchases by mail order and credit card have helped build up knowledge on people. Many Americans now destroy or shred anything that has their name or address on it.

 A professional thief used by an intelligence agency is known as a cannon.

When an important person is given security protection, the group of agents is known as a detail. In Britain the undercover agent is usually difficult to spot. In the US, like Mulder and Scully of *The X-Files*, they can stick out. They are often dressed in neat black suits and even wear dark glasses like the Men in Black!

 During the 1950s the American CIA spent a lot of money on 'spies' in Poland. The Polish knew what was going on. They took the money and used it themselves.

 The British spy Alexander Szek was reported shot dead aged only 24 in 1917. He had managed to obtain a German code book for the British during World War I. The British decided that the Germans were never to know that the enemy knew their codes. Szek was sacrificed. It is almost certain he was shot dead by another British agent.

In 1929 the USA stopped spying in peacetime. An American leader said: 'Gentlemen do not read each other's mail'!

 The American TV series *Mission: Impossible* ran from 1966 to 1972. The agents in the series worked for a US government agency called IMF: the Impossible Mission Force.

 The places where American agents train are known as 'farms'.

 The British Post Office came up with a magic bug some twenty years ago. It was called the R-12. You could put it in a telephone and then call the bug up from anywhere in the world. You could hear everything that had been said on the phone.

People who plant bugs are known as 'plumbers'. The most famous plumbers in history are those who bugged the Watergate building in Washington. The Watergate Scandal led to the resignation of the American president Richard Nixon in 1974.

 Century House, a 19-storey 1960s office block, is the home of Britain's security service. It is in the area of the Elephant and Castle in London. Taxi drivers call it the Spooks' House.

 The son of the man who helped invent cinema, Pathé, was arrested in France as a spy for the Russians in 1979. He was jailed for five years.

Female spies are either Ladies or Sisters. The ladies have the jobs which need them to work quietly at home or abroad. The sisters have the far tougher job. They are field agents who are required, if ordered, to do almost anything. In Britain there are more female spies and espionage agents than male ones.

 One of the most famous statues to a spy was that of Pole Felix Dzerzhinsky. He organized the first Soviet intelligence service, called the Cheka, in the early 1900s. His statue in Moscow was toppled after the Soviet Union fell apart in 1992.

 The Russian spy Molody was also an inventor. His car burglar alarm won a gold medal at the Brussels International Trade Fair as 'the best British entry'!

Baron von Etzdorf was born wealthy in
Germany. He began to spy for Britain in
1933, and continued the work for 12 years.
He was very successful. After World War
II his luck ran out – he lost his fortune and
ended up working at Jack's Cafe, a snack
bar in London.

 During the Korean war of the
1950s, the CIA found that their best
intelligence came from children. So
there!

 In 1968 the Israeli secret service
managed to make 200 tons of
uranium disappear from a ship in the
Mediterranean. The Israelis needed the
uranium for making nuclear weapons.

The American spy headquarters, the Puzzle Palace at Fort Meade, did not exist for many years! It was supposed to be a big secret. But it was rather obvious. It was built underground and covered 12 acres. There were aerials and antennae all over the place. The underground tunnels were packed with computers. Around it was a three-metre-high fence, with barbed wire on top. Behind this was a five-strand electrified fence. Behind this was a third fence patrolled by armed guards with dogs!

In 1960, in a brilliant operation, the Israeli secret service and commandos managed to kidnap the Nazi war criminal Adolf Eichmann in Argentina. He was put on trial and later executed by the Israelis.

 One of the problems with spies is that they can fall in love with those they are supposed to be watching. It appears to happen quite often.

 The first FBI agent to be found guilty of spying was Richard Miller in 1981. Miller may not have been that good – he often left his keys in the office door and lost his passes to secure buildings.